TRIBUTARY

ALSO BY CAREY SALERNO

Shelter

TRIBUTARY

POEMS

CAREY SALERNO

A Karen & Michael Braziller Book

PERSEA BOOKS / NEW YORK

Persea Books, Inc.
90 Broad Street
New York, New York 10004

Library of Congress Cataloging-in-Publication Data

Names: Salerno, Carey, author.
Title: Tributary / Carey Salerno.
Description: First. | New York, New York : Persea Books, Inc., [2021] | Summary: "Poems that seek to expose the struggles and failings of family and faith, the rigidity of conditional love and loyalty"—Provided by publisher.
Identifiers: LCCN 2020052509 | ISBN 9780892555291 (paperback)
Subjects: LCGFT: Poetry.
Classification: LCC PS3619.A4348 T75 2021 | DDC 811/.6—dc23
LC record available at https://lccn.loc.gov/2020052509

Book design and composition by Rita Lascaro
Typeset in Zapf Humanist and Palatino
Manufactured in the United States of America. Printed on acid-free paper.

TRIBUTARY

ORDER OF SERVICE

Processional

It's a drum. It's a drum. It's a river. It's a drum.

IMPATIENT WITH THE RIVER

xx

Speak the name of the river.   —who levels stones like hungry ears slurping gossip in the antechamber.
Speak the name of the one who stones, that lodges in the throat.
: *River*

xx

River, tell me your family name.   Coo.
River, I said I want to know it.   Fist.
River.
        I'm waiting by your wild silk spun bank with my hands open and you will place in offering what I want to fill this infertile/d ground.

xx

River— What is the name you go by?
To what, may I refer? To whom?
        What deep in your bedrock eroding?

What yawning beneath the floodwater covers awakened,
                        or in slumber drifting between the rooms of our house
            like water rippling between the stories and leaving white shadowwood,
the stairwell damp and rank? River.   Will you never speak?

xx

River.   No other name than.   No other more frustrating-
than-fuck name. River. Ephemeral.   Swear to answer

whether with snow melt, the 100-year flood, a drought I can disappear into.   Swear to telegraph,
            telepath your name, and I'll bury deep into your salt-blanched mud
                where I confess—even where I have the right to remain—here
                                    I cannot wait.

INVOCATION

River, what are you? Song of water too
pretty for the mouth, finger to scrawl.
Place we drink from, place we drown.
River above my head, daring to pour down
all the family secret, this invisible wet crown
where in the ear the words are *chunnel* and *resound*,
resound, and sound and sound, the dirty chamber
shutting the mouth, its levy, impound, its rain
hammering its round, a river above my head
making no sound, the secret in not ever out
bound, its bound, unbound. River, what are you?
River I drink from. River in which I drown.

FELLOWSHIP INVITATION

The river ran—

But rivers don't run like that.

No river can be
poured from terminal velocity
back to the dam/n(ED / ER).

Don't run like that.

INTERCESSIONS

River, invite me in.
> Strip down my body
> so that I might swallow and speak thy words.

> > > *(River hear our prayer.)*

As I am wrought in the mangrove before you,
> so is my secret path not so secret
> so are we calculable & brine-bound, River.

> > > *(River hear our prayer.)*

> > But River, if I won't ask forgiveness, you will slam the door?
> > > River!
> > > Cap the water and hot-seal the hinges
> > > nothing in nor out.

> Nothing that   *ever*   went in/out

> > No knocking on the door
> > No door

> > > *(River hear our prayer.)*

> > What is better? I ask of you, River.
> > What is better? I ask of you, Brother.

> > > *(River hear our prayer.)*

HIS NAME EVERYWHERE

These rooms I'm in—
five at once—
my voice in the aluminum duct work
███   ███   ████.

This is my father's house
ours but we don't say—

███ ████ ████

to the brother who's gone missing.
And in his absence is the sound
of his name everywhere.

I open the window to let
him out, my voice, a surge that carries
through the halls of
refusing the brother.

I practice for his absence
I practice for erasur .
███ ███ ███.

His name courses through the house
on the molecular dust,
sinking in waves to the hardwood—
I open the window and try to breathe.

Let his name out. Let me out.
No more of the secret to play,
this river deafening us.

WHEN YOU SEE SOMETHING SAY SOMETHING

i.

Not until the river reads its statement
Not until   pens its letter
Not until river   to river   to river   to river
                    it grows and becomes a thousand rivers

does the river become known as River   proper river   none of that *secret* river
none of that *don't mean shit to me*   river
                              that river creeping up all your life,

turbid brook passed on at birth—   this is what I give to you: river.
That river   *that* river is confused about where to exit.

ii.

          : backchanneling :

iii.

Am I this river   believing I'll run in both directions?
Am I this river   this tributary maker   this double speak?

iv.

I'm a twofold heart river,
a silent witness who casts down her eye and feigns not to see
the river flooding others   flooding you?

Oh are you reading this   reading all my secret   running like something free all over
the flat country?   I see you, River,

might be   on your land because rivers run like that
they do   they run   and they find   they outpace
the speed of chinwag   speed of dream   dream in which we're drowning   from
which we are most anxious to wake.

PAPER BOATS

River, it was a miracle— the first child born
after three of a changeling mother.

> I write this dispatch and fold it into a boat.
> I let it gently on top of your rushing.
> To where will it be carried?

From the mouths of these babes
shown how precious whiteness behaves—
now speak in tongues with our elders   (anxious of excommunication)
demanding to keep us sequestered like
the inmost of our secrets—made in the body, foreign body, river water
> plunged. I write them down and fold them all.

> *No more elders.*

> Paper boats. I sail them down the river. I sail them . . .
> to where will they empty? To the brine of sunk vessels
> to the wave breach and undertow
> to the saturation of the ripped page with penned—

WORDS we exchange with brethren
these WORDS we won't exchange
the first born knowing the first born
is conceived to supplant—
their very presence a denial of the body,

> a river leveling rock into stone.
> Become the stone for we will not take the rock
> say the ones who bring us into the world of rock.
> But then the myth of the rock. There is no proof—
> once the river 1000 times over has run its edge.

POSTPARTUM DEPRESSION: UNHAPPINESS, DESPAIR, SADNESS, DOWNHEARTEDNESS, MISERY, HOPELESSNESS, MELANCHOLY, DEJECTION, GLOOMINESS, SLUMP

I want to course down the Ramapo, the Wanaque,
the stream that feeds it which has no name I know
to the creek cutting the deep wood behind
your house and your garden and the chickens
being carried away by the neighbor's loose bloodhound
baying over their broke-neck bodies,
over the hundred-year flood plain
 and the crying of children who mourn the chickens
and hold the rest of the flock close to their bodies
the heat of their pounding blood speaking
the language of warmth between them.
When you call me and say you think the children are better off
without you, you think, sometimes,
I want to be the Delaware swift and direct,
tributary to your body of water, what you cry
into the shower drain if you are able to shower alone.
My sister, do not think the children cannot see how you
show them the truest kindness, as you slip a lead over the
murdering creature and tie it next to the chicken coop
as you go to fetch the neighbor to repeat
the dog has again gone loose,
your son saying, he hates the dog and you saying,
I know but try not to stay angry for too long.
And you too, sister, let go of whatever ruddy water
your body stays, run to the hard rain and let it
soak your skin with its offering; watch for me
in the water, as the river, as river rising.

WATERING THE WOOD

I cannot spill the secret that I drink—
two hands on a cup smarting the glass

I cannot release it to the wild
no fish from my hands
nor word from my mouth that would desert the body too

but for the animal thoughts I'm kept to think
I cannot spill the secret that I drink
tongue flat to quench my thirst by blackwater rain

the water table teeming beneath our home's flooded wood
my trunk full and yet downing again
the secret I cannot spill, this obligatory drink—

what will not seal me with its nothingness?
this great weight bloats my briny watered body
my blackmouth words flush and warp.

WHAT SECRETS BETWEEN SISTERS

We follow each other in what we do not say.
Careful, sister, the riverbed is wet even in August.
It will snare our footing   as it pleases
take our bodies into the cracked clayspread

~~render us bare.~~

                                        Can I trust you to save a secret?   This one
                                                        we keep but never share.

When the water pours
                        into
                                your
                                        ear   from my mouth,
remember the way of the delta and open your body
without shoaling—let that tangled rush ride straight and nurse your undertow.

            Don't let the secret break your legs from beneath you. Don't let it snare.

I won't tell it (and take down the body).
You won't tell it (and take down the body).
We will abide (and take down the body).

We will keep safe from water run astray   trough   the froth of waves
cresting, acts of speech folding neatly into the collapsing brink—
a brother's name, our heir, within the briny breast.

THE NAME GAME

We play this cloak-and-dagger
called don't speak his name.

The more we swallow him
the more ██ wants out—

a double helix spooled where the diaphragm tenses, but
the name needs a name for its detention.

We pass out from holding
down the breath the name.

This is part of the game
a private part we practice

lightly cupping air with our lips
one breath we can't breathe

in we're told it's just a game
to enter the parish

with arms raised and praise
yes like that—like you mean

it can't be a game
like you have lost your breath

and will forsake this brother
will attend the holy father

will obey instructions for his game.

OF SECRETS. SECRET RIVER. GUIDE ME THERE. GUIDE ME HOME.

Only the certain anglers know this secret river
      know the path leading to its waters
            trust in the purity
the bounty of fish gleaming
      from the frame of the Instagram feed
          What trails are ones you know
What *roads diverged in a yellow wood*
               Tell it to the river with her mouth open for the wet kiss
             Tell it to the river haunted by her bounty of fish
gleaming near the bank, spawning near the bank.
      Only the anglers know the way to her
The way to keep her hidden
The way under the bramble to her mushy bottom
The way to sink into and pull from
      her bounty of gleaming fish. Her bounty
         of secrets. Oh yes, do not forget that.
Secret river. Guide me there. Guide me home.

THE RIVER AS BODY OF WATER APPORTIONING

mind you, is flammable water, a feeding lie, a feathery neon pink hook
before which I think to open my wet jaw—

_____

But instead when the father speaks, I only wander within his speech act's startling river—
body of water apportioning—

treading with and against the current.
Secret river.   Raging river.   River's immutable spiriting of all injustice straight out
to sea—

what, really, is it made of?

_____

If I am your daughter
lost at the plunge of my burning mouth into whatever liquid was made available,

the rule that steadies even my tongue smolders—
a thumb pressed, meant to drown out these smarting embers—then you are the heat
source of my insolent speech.

           If I am the victim of the burn
                spared by the one
                who inflicts the burn,
                you are the one who hides the ointment

                that would give
                      relief. _Here it comes. Here it comes._

_____

Touch the river water, the confines of its one rushing line—
body of water apportioning, like all else in that it's unlike all else.

What comes forth from my mouth is not green now but more rushing
and not minnow but silt

~~but ash~~ but seared flesh resting atop the mind, a blanket for safekeeping, where the water will

find itself not on nor above but through.

YOU'RE NO ANGLER

Nice fallie:

fall smallie

Angler in the autumn river

green-eyed fish

Bassin' dog in the kayak

we put him in the boat

Drift cart:

fishing from a shopping cart

Flint river gig

King on gravel right there

Sweet carp rig

Why tie specific flies for Smallmouth Bass, many of which take up to a half an hour to construct, when smallies really aren't all that picky about what streamers they eat in the first place? Because the truth is the older, larger, and more educated smallmouth get, the more they will flat out refuse many flies thrown their way.
As they approach 18" and above smallmouth are just as selective if not more to size, color and presentation, both in form and function as any large trout or other predatory fish. Swim flies are very effective even in the worst, ultra-clear, low water periods.
Any serious smallmouth angler will benefit. Ask about the fall smallmouth bite.

Swim and hatch day

Small jaws syndicate

Saltwater fly fishing

A morning on glass

wishing

Giant trevally on a flip flop fly

Drum village glisten

sleddy reminiscing

Sweet carp rig

This vernacular.My house on water.In the water.On the fly.#Alldayplay these monster bass. You wouldn't try.

But sister you're no angler.

Not been the places I've been
Not seen the things that I've seen.

No, no, no. no you're no angler.

HINDSIGHT(S) OF THE SON—NOTE TO SELF

I started writing my father what I thought he wants to hear but am nearly forty and should stop behaving like the boy below his raised arm full of long plank lumber about to come down on my ass. I've lived since to avoid the lesson. *Wood slivers!* I tell my son when he walks with hand sliding along a seedy fence, *you'll get a splinter!* My father showed how to treat and dress a wound. How to tweeze. I hunched in the checkup chair with hand outstretched as he told of the boy whose brother drove a stick clean through his foot. *It was so brutal*, he said, *be thankful for your sisters*. And right then, how could I have asked, _____?

CHAGRIN BOA

Wrapped like a bangle, oh she was
a marvelous beast clung
cured in ice and sleet-slung to the branch
hanging its hang-dog low
neck over the water.

When you go out for a *nice sleddy* and find 16 feet of snake . . .

Her jaw iced open in want
of anything like that hot terrarium
air, the coarsely carpeted conservatory;
or did she strangle the impossible
cat and that's when her possessor
let her slick body into this stumbling river?

Crystallinerubbishlined river reducing the body by slights of temper-

ature and not even a high rock
of false mercy could then be slithered to
so wrapped she, yes, like a bracelet, yes,
over the water, in want of warmth
in want, perhaps, of the little feline too.

The snake once beloved which is to say *purchased*.

Or she slipped away
and the master went seeking
lantern bobbing in the percale night but she was like
to hell with this and emptied her
smooth body into the slick river.

Full of steelhead. Full of litter. This river Deluge. Called Deluge. No no called Chagrin—

What was felt by the snake
when she was placed
into the space

made by four glass walls.
What was felt by the snake
when considering the way
in which the water's siren calls.
How could she not imagine
she'd be better off drinking the silt,
surging to the corrupted name of a Frenchman—
no: the river is Native for clear water: *shagarin*.

    the Daniels Park Dam failing from ice and water both and the snake too, succumbing
to that slow death of industry, of faith, of traveling

to the Erie where she
may have found herself free
if she were to swim
fast and low, head in the shale.
American brook lamprey—
no, boa constrictor—jerked
free onto her ice block back,
warmed by coalfire in order to be stretched
to have measure taken above the snow,
to be reported.

    It's common, a person says, for someone to decide their snake has grown too big to be
a pet.

    It's not the first time, the person says, implying, too, it won't be the last.

SOME DARK ORGAN WILLING

When you strapped a fresh deer to the branch
which was the bar of their swing set,

the girls swung anyway, arched thighs around to tap
toes on the other side of its body.

Between them, a long gash in the hairy form,
left ajar for bloodletting, for words, for twiglight.

How many times did I ascend your porch stair
and let my finger do the work of pushing a button bell—

my body before you not quite what you'd expected
but what you'd accepted already as one you would not love?

Perhaps somewhere within you I'm also hanging;
my feet neatly folded beneath the mealy rope.

Perhaps one comes undone, and I dangle
there in my kandura—a mess you mind but cannot

accept the reading of. Perhaps as the red deer—whose
hooves once grazed these indigenous grasses that shimmy

in the crisp zephyrs billowing over the green plain which croons
like insects against it, as the deer sways from its bundled legs,

whose body grew longer over its days with your daughters
pumping legs in perfect communion, peering for a heart

or liver or some dark organ willing to be an offering—I am the bright
wound, open and festering, a voice beckoning you

to the renderer, a voice undressing down to itself, stumbling naked
of this tree, this fence, this greed-grown yard.

SCRIPTURE

The river's mangled idiom:

The grass in the grass is a cobra.
I can chew off more than I bite.
The water under the water is the bridge.
The bridge is a tender place   don't   count   on   already it breaks.

WATER READER INVOKES A LITTLE SHAKESPEARE

Don't wade in the absent flat of a rushing river
but hang back and settle onto its bank,
what stone spit up on the side and grass pushing through.
Let your chewy waders dry in the sunrise, the light warming first your hair.   you.   first.
When the river is rushing in its middle
seek out the secret river:
    a boulder block channeling water where brown trout tread fat and lazy awaiting the
stone fly the fruit of your cast flickering   prime lie   feeding lie
prime lie.

The river won't cease its hurry
to the afterwards place, carrying water from some home high to another one low.
Starting as the trickle of a snowcap's crown bleating,
it babbled at first like an infant.
Where once they were our whole world,
we forget how the children surprised us
mocking bird coo, lanky-leg foal, whose drunken toddling
was a drip from the thaw now galloping wild before us.
But soft, what light through yonder window
breaks? It is the east, and ███,
the fly fisher, you will not be my son.

SONG FOR THE RIVER LIKE A TONGUE

Into into into don't walk me down into
Into into into don't want to be walked down
into
Into the river yes it's cruel
into into into
Sings the river a name for you
Into into into but don't walk down
into
the river sallow with rusted leaves
the river rank onto your knees
Don't want to walk   into into into
into the river like a tongue
its language forked leaving us dumb
Into into into don't walk me down into
the river   what did you do   don't walk me

Don't wet me.
Don't speak for me.
River, please,
sing your name to me . . .

BAPTISM WITH A POND IN IT

I saw my sister resurrect, wet
and shining, and applauded and spun
to sprint up the hill from the pond
but the water, sweet dumb
and warm still, and the preacher's thumb
and finger clamped, pushed my body into what
was made to bring me closer to—

body of water apportioning where
the only water roaring was
quick to suffocate my face.
I closed my eyes and searched for
the river and there only could place
my father drunk, unspooling me like a
carpet into the water, his arm a firm cane
forcing the body in.

But how I wanted to stay below,
void of sound and drumswole cello,
void of white bright. The body buoyant bellow
and effervescing halo,
an ocean swelling the capillary and marrow.

What was the sin, for what to atone
as a child in drenched Sunday robes who wept.
The hope of transformation, and not for any joy
nor salvation, dear father—what arrives
suddenly in a dirty moat, a preacher's sodden bay?
Even the fish won't take up residence. Let us pray.
What's left in the water will not wash away.

MEN CREAM WHITE BELLS

I hear church bells	I	bells white I hear
white church bells	white	white church white
church bells like	church	cream like bells church bells
white ice cream men	white	men white as ice
calling me up	calling	house I step from calling
step from the sodden house	step	the sodden
into the rain of	into	into
the music of	the	bells of music of the rain
churchbells	church	churchbells white church-
white churchbells	white	bells blaring
blaring the	blaring	of whether he is risen
bell	bell	killing of the question
calling forth sermon	calling	clear crown of thorns
calling us	calling	thanking god for the
to our knees before	to	jesus on his cross
jesus on his cross	jesus	to our knees before
thanking god for the	thanking	calling us
clear crown of thorns	clear	calling forth sermon
killing of the question	killing	bell
of whether he is risen	of	blaring the
bells blaring	bells	white churchbells
churchbells white church-	churchbells	churchbells
bells of music of the rain	bells	the music of
into	into	into the rain of
the sodden	the	step from the sodden house
house I step from calling	house	calling me up
men white as ice	men	white ice cream men
cream like bells church bells	cream	church bells like
white church white	white	white church bells
bells white I hear	bells	I hear church bells

THE RIVER'S ANXIETY IS THE RIVER UNDERGROUND

Don't question it. Don't think of it. Don't let you get in front of you.
Don't question it. Don't think of it. Don't let you get in front of you.
Don't question it. Don't think of it. Don't let you get in front of you.
Don't question it. Don't think of it. Don't let you get in front of you.
Don't question it. Don't think of it. Don't let you get in front of you.
Don't question it. Don't think of it. Don't let you get in front of you.
Don't question it. Don't think of it. Don't let you get in front of you.
Don't question it. Don't think of it. Don't let you get in front of you.
Don't question it. Don't think of it. Don't let you get in front of you.
Don't question it. Don't think of it. Don't let you get in front of you.
Don't question it. Don't think of it. Don't let you get in front of you.
Don't question it. Don't think of it. Don't let you get in front of you.
Don't question it. Don't think of it. Don't let you get in front of you.
Don't question it. Don't think of it. Don't let you get in front of you.
Don't question it. Don't think of it. Don't let you get in front of you.
Don't question it. Don't think of it. Don't let you get in front of you.
Don't question it. Don't think of it. Don't let you get in front of you.
Don't question it. Don't think of it. Don't let you get in front of you.
Don't question it. Don't think of it. Don't let you get in front of you.
Don't question it. Don't think of it. Don't let you get in front of you.
Don't question it. Don't think of it. Don't let you get in front of you.
Don't question it. Don't think of it. Don't let you get in front of you.
Don't question it. Don't think of it. Don't let   it   get in front of you.

BAPTISM WITH A RIVER IN IT

Pull the girls by the hair to the river.
        Make them speak its water, that sweet dumb speech.

Pull the girls by their heat-pocked hair.
        They open murky mouths for its secret
but no secret there.

        Oh, oh no   no scripture sleeping upright in her chair.
        Oh no, no   heretics to lunge forth in evening prayer
                who were born of the dear father who pulls
girls to the river to wash scorched hair

in the sweet secret of his heat dumb name
        coalwash that rises from still water
            wash it from lips, part, and carry the water away

as the body of our bodies, my sisters, the river will accept
        the secret not a secret but a secret deep in the bed
of another life to where our heirs will never be lead

        where we gallop to the river   to be drenched:
        in our dresses   beneath the father who demands
commitment   against our will   to rip from the root our brother's
name

SAYS THE RIVER TO HER PATRIARCHY

to explain how
a tributary
becomes a river
there isn't a way
but for the tributary
to deny it—
I deny
the very river
I deny the paying
of tribute
grow up, say
the men
in my life
men who
gave me life
when I am
already the river
I say
I am the river
I say
I am grown I say
listen
to my rushing
I say
you will stay
until I've finished
my rushing

TATTOOS

To the child I try to explain what the water takes, how
it will claim the temporary tattoo but not the hand
to which it's applied. It will drink the dye from clothes,
push its way into the permeable cells of skin,
plump arms and thighs, neck and hair the sponge receiving.

And how wanting its wetness is want to wash it in—
the little molecules against penetrable membranes
hurrying their exchange like the trite dialogue
looping from our minds to our mouths.
I just said what you think I just said I think

is what I said to the child when he cried at the loss of the humpback whale stamp
to the water when the water accepted what he supplied
willingly, unwillingly—what is there is no difference.

CATCH AND RELEASE

bury the horned branch
plunged into the riverbed

burrs hitching a ride
one by one they eddy and disappear

the way we receive a rumor then release it

where deep in the bed is a rose bush growing
flower and pricker together

subaquatic
tangled as roots of the aspen

are you going to keep writing the names of trees?
the way molecules of water take the form of their container—

legs in the water, for what are you casting?
legs on the bank, for whom are you watching?

swoop
ripple

i see fish rise against the current, flicking ruddy tails
the way they do when caught, when released

WE KNOW THAT SOUND TRAVELS BETTER OVER WATER

To the river that is our history, I come reluctantly; and to the river that ran
      suddenly through me, a man-made damn opening to release its man-made lake;
to the dividing of peoples—where thru the divide I am no *navigatrix*.

Stand on the river and be sure of foot. It's no short order.
Drink from the river with no gag from its force. Wade into its border.
Raft above until the water sinks the wood and wears its rope.

Sweet river, how I hate your very presence
      the beauty of your misery and its need for constant explanation
Well, once upon a time there was a man and his son,

and the story is a lie in the form of a fairytale which too is a lie, but a sweeter lie to be
sure, I said to the boy I grew within me, within the very river too.

I see the rock raising round the eddy. I feel the swift debris gather in
      the sieve of my fingers, the soaking wool sleeve.
How can I abide it, care for it, carry the damned branches back into

the deep wood, wet and murky, no place for a child no place for a lover nor
trade for daughter nor sisters? How can I shout into the river and the shout
refract to where a boy runs wild to catch the words on either side?

Dear, great river growing. Dear, *they will not replace us.* Dear great river part of my life
unfailingly,
      to where may I climb to pike your water? Or do you teach me how to teach
my children to swim, to wade, to scoop from you the most precious

shining hate, what deepens you, river, that lies in the black bedrock, to step into your
dubious base and loose the shoe, to come back with waders and a rod
to fish from you, to eat from you, to be nourished by you, to carry

your story inside them, a canyon in the body. In the body. In the body.
      In the body of you, river, is an answer and what I mean by answer is an end.
Even if out to sea, and we may very well go to sea, there will be an end—

WHY WE DON'T PRAY, RIVER

River   you are
    not   through
                    me

but of me

                        River
                        you are
        not   what
                    swerves
                        but

            what
            seals
    this body   River

    to our body rivers

Message

a salt on your salt on your wound agape

THE RIVER BEGINS TO FALL

You can speak to the water but cannot make it answer,
deliver your report as you do to the mushy grave
of your grandmother, and every time, the same scene emerges: casket cranking into the
black tinsel below the electric green astroturf, the watery lock of a flooded gold vault. The
flamboyant soil.

It was spring, the Arlington earth soaked and a
bouquet of red roses cradled on my elbow overripe with rain.

You cannot make the dry body answer to the word slurry running off the grass glittering
into the eddy.

Scream at the river and it will return this act
at the voice's hard rock
where deafening water gallons out into the frothing plunge pool

The black leather of my heels kept getting sucked into
the snowmelt loam above the graves on which we
gathered and shook.

where even the waterfall retreats when it reaches that dull lard-knife ledge
seeking instead the dumb mouth of its river—
the every why for which there is no answer—
speak it to the river, lean in and say to the stumbling water all your tarry sludge.

The March rains wet our lips with their callous skins,
and we swallowed back our words, filled what's emptied.
And again.

GIVEN HORSE

No man ought to looke a geuen hors in the mouth.

    —John Heywood, from *A Dialogue of the Effectual Prouerbs in the English Tongue*
      Concerning Marriage (1546)

I will not look him in the
mouth   I will not look him in
the woman   No woman ought
no man   None ought inspect the teeth
of this horse unless this horse be the gift
of trouble   be the gift of burden wrapped
in glitter strewn   be the horse the kind
that kick hard when you feed it   I look it in the mouth
and see it deep cave of secret   it telltale 21lb heart
I look the horse in the mouth and you watch   you
can't stop me cant stop   me seeing it   teeth rot out
Ya that horse is gifted but sure   doesn't mean it's a gift
I'm not about to let you tell me   where I open my eyes   where no woman
ought.   What   we know about these rules, Heywood. That *geuen hors,*
"Heyword."
That gift of meat and bone, hey word   That princess neigh and swagger, hey / word
That bloody mouth hacking the bit red with terror telling me not to stare, hey
word
What do you know, hay.Werd.

RIVER WHO ABSCONDS

I want to disappear
I want to walk into the unbeached sands
I think I'll see for miles
because
I'm told it is all sand
like the creek
cutting a deep bank
beyond the backwood—
beyond the America-
n flag dotting these trailer awnings—
creek not quite deep enough

        creek I could not sink into.

This wanting
I cannot outdo
like the eddy
between two rocks deepening
as it blends
my jet fare
for what *a girl can
only wish*
to that indifference
is the difference
to the sand, the silt,
the river that won't

        cut deeply enough to drown in.

Did I say *river* already?
how it refuses this new martyr?
a little lioness
in the water
body that cannot
drown
that cannot cut down

the children
pinched scruffs in my mouth
I'll open arms
embrace them with my river—
my breast
blood this river,
vein silt,
eddy death.
I say yes

I believe that
I am guilty
of this charge.

SILENT CONFESSION

I always wanted to be able to write someone out of my will
strike the name, recall it from the flameful bush
to be principal enough to say
I always wanted to say, "I took you out of the will!"
to one of my sons or daughters.

So when you toddled up to where I was fixing
the classic car, bleeding the clutch, pressing down the ball
of my foot with the intact power of my body,
I'm sure you weren't alarmed
when I craned my neck out the cracked window and bellowed,

You're not getting this car!

ISAAC & ABRAHAM

Where are you? Here I am. Where are you? Here I am.

A RIVER KNOWS ITS ECHO CANNOT ANSWER

River, I shout into you expecting an echo.
I press my lips to your surface in want of traction.
I open my palm and plunge it into your murky bed.

River, why won't you unwater that which I am seeking?
Why won't you raise the stone that skimmed your surface?
Please speak back. Whether with flooding. Whether with drought.

River, come change long in this season of brevity.
Take the house and its mewling cat. Take its drinkers of water.
Rise with a howl over the land and consume the way I flip

up the faucet handle and assume your body already running over my hand.
Take me over, river, and rinse, leave bland. Or leave me silted and undressed.
Leave me without breath at the very bottom where I burrow

in the covers of your bed. I shout into you and expect an echo,
River. So, echo!
echo echo. answer. echo echo dread.

RIVER REDUCED TO MONOLITH

River, your story isn't one of a babbling brook
       nor are you a baby, crawling through the countryside
       nor snake on your belly, slinking between rock.
You are not my vein full of water.

River, you are not a brook so infantile as only can prattle.
       You are no polliwog, nor must you grow up
       to be a briny version of yourself. Nor must you prove
your worth in stone smoothing, fish hoard, nor quickening.

River, you are not one animal, poisonous nor benevolent,
             but rather no animal, a mother to the mothers, to all animals
                 including this imperfect human on the other
          end
          of a poem—you are the string, perhaps, that pulls
     two apparitions together, through the picture of yourself:
                    the
                    paper chain of
                    dress donning
                    dolls or little
                    faceless men.
But River, you don't need to be a semblance!
       You are not the reflection in mirrored water but the water bright with ripple.

River, unhook your bra, raise your flags proudly
and welcome whatever is dumped into you with more wild rushing.
       Take in and in all of the secret: what is spoken at you
       & what you can never speak back. Carry it into the body
              you believe long ahead of you, the body you are steady
             ambling to meet—the body you've grown into—and widen
and deepen and still find there is a wealth of pleasure to be had.
Roughen up the bank and yes, take down a few trees
              with the storm, show you're no trifle, no tributary
no sweet babe learning to swim, but a grand, cold-blooded vertebrate wrought

—already.

SICK HORSE

Girls, you can bring that horse to water—
sick horse, desert-mouth horse,
horse painted to slick sedimentary rock.

Bring that horse to water, you can girl—
horse bit-grinding
horse you really gotta drag
red stencil, skinny-ass horse.

That horse to the water, bring him.
Girls when it   lie down there that
belly on the bank
don't forget to praise

to stroke the hoary mane
and coo at him
sweetly bray his name.
Don't forget to praise who made this horse

And made for you the walk
And made for you the bridle
And made for you the cracked earth in want of water
And made for you this river
And made for you this labor

Yank on that bridle, Bitches, yank it
Yank that horse and force its head down
Prove you cannot make the man drink

LONE WOLF: A LETTER

I said that's it.
I gave you everything I know you want
but all you do is shirk me.
I'm tired of these Muslims
coming in and shooting up the place.
I'm skipping my godchild's christening to lay
grace at the church's concealed weapons assembly.
We've been meaning to go…
and this has got to stop.

It makes me sick the way these people
are blowing everything up.
When in that letter you wrote these shooters are deranged white men whose faith is
firearms,
I guess you meant me?
Pfff.
I'm no murderer! I'm no thief!
All I want is to snipe
whoever's trying to kill me first.
It's my right
now. My thirst.
I'll have a gun. I'll have my thrill.
everywhere. anywhere.
I'm done,

███.

RIVER EPHEMERAL

River, why did you lead me to you
                              when there is no water
                              not to drink nor drown in
                              not to stare into and see this whiteness
                                        to see past the whiteout of whiteness
                    snowsquall into the rushing water which does not warm
not by the sun nor by my breath   not by the school of trout huddling near the bank
no trout in this stream   no water   no stream

I want to peel back this fish skin and reveal some new pigment
here on the bank   where it is not safe to disrobe
                                        nor to have these fluted organs in my
                                        body
To whom do I say this?
River dried up,
          river a bed of rock between me and another wood.
                                        River with no shadow, no
                                        sand in which to sink,
                                        river with no body.
              River of form and formless.

THE BINDING OF

Behold the fire and wood
but where is the river to test it,
to walk into and drown within?
Where is the man who carries his son to the reservoir
and buries him in its old blood clay?

Father, I lurched into the shed and there you were
like a knife shrieking upon its file,
the wet 2x4 in your arm towering above my brother.
Will you take me also to that river?
Whatever wrong he's committed must also be mine.

Whatever my love for him, a wickedness, slick in your eyes—
I would rather drown in it—the blackwater mouth,
its lone ghost groan,
smoothing me into your sentient stone—
or perhaps Brother, ferry me away to the summit alter,

lay me down upon its hay-tentacled rock, raise the ready dagger
and when Adonai calls, do not even answer
Here I am.

WISHBONE

Black wishbone white wishbone

Which wishbone   bone

My wishbone

None my wishbone

Open me and find blackbone below the deep red pool

Open me and find the dark intention

Open me and find the ghost my father carries

Gnawing at the bone white   Black bone

Which bone is my bone

White bone   We all bleed   We all white bone

Open me and find my father scrubbing black from these bones

Open me and find him straining his body into the brush bristles

He makes an art project of his daughter his blank canvas his blank bone

Open me and see where he pours in the bleach bone

Which bone is my bone

No bone is my bone

Black wishbone   Black wish   Black wish the wishbone the white wishbone

The white bone   Wishbone   Open me and see I have both breastbones

Open me and see I own black and white I made

Both wishbones   Wish and bone   I am the wishmaker and one who hears the wish

All the wishes in these bones

My wishes in these bones   My bones

No, not my bones, my father force-feeding me the bones

He said clean them with your tongue   He showed me

The way to white wash our bones   To keep them family bones   To quicklime

The bones in a box   in my hands   stored in the closet

For my children   to be taken out to show

Not for splitting these bones and only for us to split these bones. The story of the bones

Black and white. The story of wishbone. Tell the wish without pulling apart the bone

They say   Hold black wishbone and white wishbone   One in each hand

Place them behind the back and ask which bone

The answer is both bones   The answer is no bones   Your answer is the answer

Always the answer   for years the answer   all answers that answer

White bone   Black bone   I tell you your wish before you break

for Monica Hand

FOR ALL BUT .0001%

we remain uncertain of
the content of clan secrets

     in all the earth's rivers
     so little water is the river

we process by touching finger to
in this manner of a child

     and the molecules evaporate
     as does our matriarch—early to menopause

we're splashing hands
in a bucket in the perennial garden in the land that awaits the dubious fates of rain
     we stroke the blossom of a moonwhitemoon flower,
     mouths stumbling *brother*

  all but for the word are we dumb

IDIOMATIC WATER

a fish out of water a tall drink of water above water as a duck takes to water back water be as oil and water be dead in the water be in deep water be in hot water be like a fish out of water be like oil and water be water off a duck's back be water under the bridge between wind and water big drink of water blood in the water blood is thicker than water (?) blow out of the water blow someone out of the water body of water bread and water by hell or high water carry fire in one hand and water in the other carry water carry water for (someone) cast bread upon the waters come hell or high water come on in come on in, the water's fine! could talk under water couldn't pour water out of a boot cut water off dead in the water deep water dip my toe in the water dull as dishwater fish in troubled waters fish out of water, a foo-foo water get head above water and have head above water get in(to) deep water get in(to) hot water go through fire and water have just one oar in the water joy water laughing water like a fish out of water like water off a duck's back long drink of water make mouth water make one's mouth water the mill cannot grind with water that is past mouth-watering muddy the water muddy the waters murky waters not hold water of the first water oil and water pay the water bill plowing water pour cold water on pour cold water on something pour oil on troubled water pour oil on troubled waters spend money like water still waters run deep to take to like a duck to water test the water test the waters through hell and high water throw cold water on throw out the baby with the bath water throw the baby out with the bath water toilet water tread water troubled waters turn someone's water off turn water off uncharted waters under water untested waters water down water one's cheeks water over the dam water under the bridge watering hole wonder water won't hold water woofle-water wozzle-water you can lead a horse to water you can lead a horse to water but you can't make it drink you can lead a horse to water, but you can't make it drink you never miss the water till the well runs dry

AFFIRMATION OF FAITH

Secret bigot
Hush-hush ♥
Do not pray 4 me

—Angler via Text Message

RIVERHEAD IN THE RIVER

There's nothing to wash your speech:
not the rain between your city and mine
not the flood water's glimmer on the hundred-year plain

There's nothing to stop the deep red
staining the shoremuck of the riverbank, the sun bleaching out our sightline.
My head beneath the current fills, its serrated fishtail swirling

Terrorist, rapist, criminal
the black mouth melody of millions of gallons recitating.
The father of, are you not? The sister. And the brother too?
                    God damn the lowly creature we refer to as *us*:

                         Little living, who just wants to feel better in the water
                                        not wrung out
                                  whipped and puckered,
        not some headless snake slung low over this slow arm—a mud-hardened tributary.

WHITEWASH

The family farm
Our dairy barn
Strip the interior

Whitewash
Debris into byre gutter
Quicklime the walls

As in the tree's trunk must be painted to protect
its fruit-bearing as in the girl
was told by her parents not to visit the codeword: heights
The girl was told by her friends' parents not to date the boy
not dare part the milkmaid thighs.
Mix the limewash and dip the brush, the tree trunk must
be painted. If it is to bear fruit. If it is to withstand the frost.
If it is to stay away from the code: bad neighborhood just north of here.
If it is to do as we would want. The girl must be washed
and coated, the lime of our words a shell. It's the best we can do
to keep her, to keep her bearing fruit, to keep her
one of the orchard, whitewashed.

To camouflage, oh! We owe whitewash a debt
Especially in winter
Hid us from the enemy
Hid us deep in our anemic villages and cities
Hid us deep in the white of its whiteness

Song of whitewash
Inside the cocoon of white of whiteness

A game in which one side of players
fails to score at all

THE FATHER CASTS FOR GABRIEL

What message did you mean for me?

What hot night twisted in whitewashed sheets?

       What image of my son to haunt me—
                  he in a beard and dress.
         He in his first pair of waders.

                          Follow me and I will make you fishers of men,
          the prophet says unto likely disciples who drop their soaking nets.
          Follow me and I will make you fishers of men, we chant (recant)
but show me where there is righteousness beyond our vision of white legs burrowed in
                                  the garden of
                                  Gethsemane,
       or perhaps in the pearlescent moonstone desert mistaken for this garden?
              (Of all the temptations, stones into bread I love the most.)

The driving of dull stakes into iridescent wrists—

                      what message did you mean for me?

    What to be told by a man that a man may rise from the dead—how belief is built by
this foreshadowing: Coppola's oranges pressed against the front teeth or a conjuring of
                   Lazarus, *coming forth* from his grave.

My son twists the white-hot sheet into a crown.

He burns more brightly in my body than anger's tallest candle.
                    In a dress.
                    In his first waders.

      I cannot untangle them.

What message did you mean for me?

Please. Come back.

GLORY BE TO THE OFFERING

Much of my life I've spent begging.
Much of my life slavering
over the offering plate
passed before me—a feeble weight
on the end of my neighbor's starch-cuffed arm.

That blue of me becoming
a blue undone, the debt
of cloud cover,
debt of
the empty blue-bleach hand. The debt
of blue to the soil
from which it stretches.

How the dish sings against the nickels flung,
its sun gold rim brimming,
the sound as empty of oaths as it is full of grubby hands.

I tilt my chin to the chapel dome and mouth the words
Glory be.

I open my shirt—
one thousand times one hundred angels wringing out their sleet-soaked wings—their
psalm lifting from the pocket on my crocus chest, its stamen & pistil.
I am not one of them.
Will I be one of them?

NO RIVER, BUT THE FRAGMENT OF WHAT ONCE CONTAINED IT

if I were meant to read, *the lord*
is my Shepard I shall not
want aloud at the service
from the sticky pulpit
without mentioning
our scripture's wanton deceit—
a plummeted water jar of
river   water   shaling   limerock,
lashing its will onto the earth,
its ridges mealy and razor—

then like the river, I'm what my sister once
told me, "always running away,"
and since then I've wondered if that too
is the calculus of god, or if what
she really means is toward
like the meander of a diamondback
river, snaking south for parched rock,
the black bottom ocean,
her fear of me something radiant
instead of something feral, curled
in the dark corner of my father's
childhood bedroom on the day
of our grandmother's funeral,

a day our brother would not attend
to view the body, to read the prescriptive psalm,
to leer at the slick-face pastor
to accept the duty of death photographer,
and if he were a boat and I
river rushing   through   and through   and through
deepening and pilfering what I will,
the salt and stick and marsh
of my opening is where
our sister's words become sediment,

where the call and response is water,
more and more water,
a true blood brother moored at my mouth,
hearing only of the death
and nothing of how the family
charted the maternal shipwreck—
knee deep in the marsh
hands splayed
water rushing through the long knives
of our sunken words.

When we were younger,
my brother bade me climb
onto the crown of our house
and jump down to the grasslit earth.
You can do it, he said, but even then
I knew the tone of disbelief.
Now, I hear my sister's words.
I see in the water jar our first Babel
where we swam in the body
of our bodies' vocal lurching.

I see how we cannot go back.
How I can never gather all
the shards up by hand, nor assume
reconstruction of the glass,
nor drink the splintered water.
Our bodies are a body of animals,
the land is stuck and gorged below us.
Let us meet here and sing in mourning,
let us drift and kiss the surface of the estuary.
My brother. My sister. I am all done
running if I were ever running. I am no river,
but the fragment of what once contained it,
what once fit us together, what now reminds
upon every glance of the thing irreparably broken.

Benediction

My church is in the river. My church is in the woods.

BLESSING THE RIVER, BLESSING FOR BOUNTY

Let me remember the river, its sickcalm rock sliding beneath the foot,
its years having wandered in this wood I keep to myself
fixing flies on its bank within a bellow of mosquitos;
I work the thread through the eye of a hook, I work the bobber, xxx I call them xxx

In the water, my reflection, my signature on the line of a document I cannot read,
like the one of me leaning
over the side of our aluminum boat made swift with its motor affixed to the hull.
Looking in I wondered how deep the water then, how secret

the muck beneath it, how deep the water now
and everything in between what is foreign to me, what I'm waiting for to catch the line,
us together in the boat, something to start a conversation in this quiet.
You pray be still to encourage the fish to draw nearer
I pray to whip the lash on the river and cast them out.

Our bobbers white and cherry on either side of the boat—
starboard, the other one less interesting than starboard.
Who says *starboard* for little thing such as ours. The formality. Let's just be together on the
water, while it laps at the basin, carrying our weight and will,

this water we call still but which cannot be anything but, where my open mouth
appears just as black as it is in the mirror, a cave of words I didn't say
and now cannot say to you, my father, of the same planet, same state
even, of the same interest, who taught me how to pluck these fish

from the water. I wander this wood seeking you, a dad and a father's child,
something simple as that in the bedrock, on the riverbank, in the headwaters here
where I hold the caught fish to the light, raising him to my eye, tilting
its belly toward the bright white and illuming its greens and pinks,

its *ancient wallpaper*, slipping from its mouth the lures he had the most grace not to
swallow.
I hold him up and then sink him back to the stream, hands submerged.
I watch his tail flit and twitter. He, too, wants away.
Let us leave this place.

Notes

"You're No Angler" draws influence from the song "Nann" by Trick Daddy, featuring Trina and cites text directly drawn from an Instagram post by @schultzoutfitters

"Baptism with a Pond in It" draws influence from Michael Waters' poem, "Horse."

"Paper Boats" draws the line "no more elders" from "To Plath, To Sexton" by Jean Valentine

"The Binding of" draws from a story from the Book of Genesis in the Bible, particularly this passage: "He said, 'Take your son, your only son Isaac, whom you love, and go to the land of Moriah, and offer him there as a burnt offering on one of the mountains that I shall show you.'" —Genesis 22:2

"Wishbones" is written in conversation with Lorna Simpson's *III (Three Wishbones in a Wood Box)*, 1994

Acknowledgments

Gratitude to the editors of the following publications where these poems first appeared. This collected work would certainly not be possible without their generous support and encouragement.

New England Review: "Baptism with a Pond in It"

Los Angeles Review: "River Ephemeral" and "Water Reader Invokes a Little Shakespeare"

Quarterly West: "Given Horse"

The Literary Review: "Says the River to Her Patriarchy" and "The Name Game"

The American Poetry Review: "Blessing the River, Blessing for Bounty"

Interim: "His Name Everywhere" and "Post-partum Depression/Unhappiness, Despair, Sadness, Downheartedness, Misery, Hopelessness, Melancholy, Dejection, Gloominess, Slump"

Spillway: "Of Secrets. Secret River. Guide Me There. Guide Me Home"

The Eloquent Poem, edited by Elise Paschen (Persea, April 2019): "River Channeling in the Ear"

Alaska Quarterly Review, "Sick Horse"

The Idaho Review, "River Who Absconds"

Enormous helpings of gratitude to the amazing team at Persea Books for their support of this work with particular thanks to my editor, Gabriel Fried. Thank you for believing in these poems. I appreciate all of you and all you do for your artists.

To Anne Marie Macari, I owe deep and abiding gratitude for your support and encouragement of these poems and of my poetry in general. Thank you and big love to you. And, too, to Shara McCallum, Adrian Matejka, Kristen Case, Shana Youngdahl, and Jeffrey Thomson. The enormity of your generosity, in particular, is profound and certainly influenced the development of this book in a multitude of ways.

To my AJB team and family of artists, thank you always for your care, friendship, and inspiration. Thank you for asking me about my writing, for validating this part of me.

Thank you, poets, for our community. May it grow more broadly and deeply than any river we might ever come to know.